Acknowledgments

Thanks must go to my daughters Michelle and Lousia who without their help and encouragement this book might not have been written.

Also thanks must go to The Rev. Bob Younger who so kindly illustrated the poems.

Copyright @ Jill Nutbeem2008

The right of Jill Nutbeem to be identified as Author of this work has been asserted in accordance with the Copyrights, Designs and Patents Act 1988.

All rights reserved. No part of this book may be reprinted or reproduced or utilised In any form or by any electronic, mechanical or other means, now known or hereafter Invented, including photocopying and recording, or in any information storage or retrieval system, without permission in writing from the author.

Published by Jill Nutbeem

Printed and bound by The Knaphill Print Co Ltd.

Title
Smile A While poems for children

ISBN No: 978-0-9558833-0-9.

Smile A While

Poems for Children

by
Jill Nutbeem

Contents

		Page
1.	The Birthday	2
2.	The Wishing Well	4
3.	The Playroom	5
4.	The Cut Log	6
5.	Teddy Bear Footprints	8
6.	The Symphony Of The Trees	10
7.	The Cat	12
8.	Sea Mist	13
9.	Imagine	14
10.	Ronnie The Mule	16
11.	Fireworks	17
12.	Minnie The Mouse	18
13.	Mildred The Duck	19
14.	Cat Nap	20
15.	Teddy Bear Blues	21
16.	Little Brown Rabbit	22
17.	Eagle Eyes	23
18.	Dancing Feet	24
19.	Pepe	25
20.	Friendship	26
21.	Monkey	28
22.	The Tiger And The Elephant	30
23.	A Tasty Treat	31
24.	Head To Head	32
25.	Distant Lands	33
26.	The Sweet Shop	34
27.	The Supermarket Trolley	35
28.	The Steam Train	36
29.	The Library Book	37
30.	The Settee	38
31.	The Rocking Horse	40
32.	The Smallest Sparrow	41
33.	Tiptoe Down The Stairs	42
34.	A Bedtime Prayer	44
35.	The Frog And The Fairy	45
36.	Abreast Of The Times	46
37.	The Enchanted Garden	48
38.	The Little Red Train	50
39.	And So They Came	51
40.	The Scarecrow	52
41.	The Rocking Chair	54
42.	My Hottie	56
43.	The Deliciously Amusing Fang-Toothed Cat	58
44.	The Dressing Up Box	60
45.	The Dandelion Clock	61
46.	The Rock Pool	62
47.	The Tooth Fairy	64
48.	Daisy Bright	65
49.	Playtime	66

The Birthday
by me aged 10¹/₂

Eighty years old was my Great-Grandad last week,
and we had a party as a special treat
The day was bright and sunny, as birthdays should be,
with a promise of lots of good things for tea.

My Great-Grandad look smart in a suit and bow tie,
as we opened his presents side by side.
Aunt Mavis had sent him a brand new jumper,
which made my Great Grandad look even plumper!

The games and frolics after tea were brill
and my sister and I were never still.
I won the "pass the parcel"
and my aunt called me a little rascal –
I don't know why she called me that,
*as I thought **she** was big and fat!*

Tea was the bestest thing for me,
as I loved the jelly and ice-cream, you see.
There were sausage rolls and vol-au-vents galore –
though some of it landed on the kitchen floor!
My dog Whisky cleared up the mess,
then wondered why she was over-stressed.

The cake was a wondrous thing to behold;
it was blue and yellow, with a tale to be told.
A friend of my mum's, a baker by trade,
had nearly lost the cake, following a raid.

*The day ended on a happy note.
It was the best one yet, according to vote.
My cousins all left in their Dormobile,
leaving the dogs to eat a very scrumptious meal.*

*I was tired as I climbed the stairs to bed.
There was little more to say, that had not been said.
I was asleep as my head touched the pillow,
dreaming of birthday cakes in brilliant yellow.*

The Wishing Well

Sitting deep within the hedge,
The old stone wishing-well sat on the edge
Of bluebell wood; of childish haunts
That never could my spirits daunt.
Flanked by bluebells, primroses, and ivy,
The wishing-well stood as a monument
Of by-gone days when children so lively
Would run the lane and throw in coins of charity.
Moss now clings to the ancient stone,
And it has a whimsical air all its own.
Many times, as a child, I would run to the well
Before disappearing into the woodland dell.
The wishes it granted were varied and few,
As of the wishing-well only few knew.
Its bucket had gone, as had its rope,
And its bottom was dry, where water once slopped.
In its dying state the wishing-well held high its head,
And nestled more comfortably in its bed.
It had but one more wish to grant
To a young child, for whom it would always enchant.

The Playroom

My place of wonder, my place of dreams;
nothing in here is what it seems.
My scooter becomes a dragon bold,
who slew the wicked king stone cold.

My dolls' house is a royal palace
where there is always joy, and no malice.
The princes and princesses are lovely to see –
until I'm called to come out for tea.

A settee's in here, close to the side of the room,
which makes a good site from which to zoom
my paper aeroplanes, to fly to the moon
and bring back green cheese, very soon.

There's a fish tank in here, and stick insects, too,
making some people think they've come to a zoo.
A fireplace of green sets the right scene
for a display of relics of old that have been.

My hand-made library of an orange box
houses just about everything, including rocks.
I'm a dab hand at digging in likely spots,
which accounts for the archaeological finds of pots.

All these are displayed on window-sill grand,
all dusted and labelled by my fair hand.
For my friends who call, there's a small display
which they can enjoy without any dismay.

The doors are now closed on this magic playroom,
as my growing-up years came in to illumine.
How the fantasy world was only a step away
to what I would become one day.

The Cut Log

As the mighty log was hewn in two,
it was time to see what man would do.
Into the jungle clearing the foresters came,
ready to do their work again.

The log that was hewn was hoisted high
and carried to the river nearby.
Joining hundreds of others, with a sigh,
it was jostled along on its way by and by.

The river was kind and gave up its prize,
such was the ebb and flow of the tide.
Into the great sawmills our log went,
to be ready for shipment wherever sent.

The great ships came to carry the load
of dozens of logs that were in the hold.
Our log shuddered to find himself not very bold.

The journey across the sea seemed to take forever,
and the log that was hewn felt as light as a feather.
At last the journey was over, the ship emptying its load.
As the log waited in line, it felt cold.
From a comfortable jungle climate
he hadn't even got raiment.

Suddenly, what he was waiting for happened:
a man's voice came alongside,
and before he was dampened,
he was taken along for a ride.

The journey came to an end at last.
The long line of logs swam before his eyes
as he relinquished all his jungle ties.

Into a workshop he was quickly swept.
He was so exhausted he silently wept.
A man appeared out of the gloom,
and ran his eyes over the log that was hewn.
"This is just what I want," he exclaimed.
"Cabinet maker by trade," he explained;
"I can make a beautiful bureau out of this."

The log felt he would burst with pride
as he went with the man on his final ride.
The bureau was lovely, as was expected.
The log was jubilant in his new-found status
for, at last, he was respected.

Teddy Bear Footprints

In the rockery, beneath the tree,
tiny footprints could be seen by you and me.
The bearer was unknown –
but obviously they hadn't grown!

We waited each and every day to see what, or
whom, would pass our way.
There was no sign of friend or foe,
and so we had to let the story go.

Rather than fairy prints at the bottom of the dell,
we had other footprints there as well.
It was stranger than fiction, or so it seemed,
to have a mystery story that might have been.

Each day the footprints would appear,
but never when there was anyone near.
It became a legend in the neighbourhood,
and nobody would pass that way to the wood.

Then one dark and wintry night
the footprints gave us all a fright;
For there, etched out in the frozen snow,
were footprints so many they were row by row.

Clearly seen in the crispness of a winter's day,
they certainly hadn't gone away.
To find the owners now was the clear intent,
as we needed to know from where they came and went.

Then into the story came a strange old gent,
who claimed to know where the footprints went.
He said he would show us very soon –
but it would have to be by the light of the moon.

It was dark one night as he re-appeared;
he hadn't forgotten us, as we had feared.
"Come with me," he beckoned with a wave of his hand,
"and I will now show you a very merry band."

In silence we walked together, afraid of what we might see,
when suddenly the old man stopped by the side of a tree.
"Look into the hole in the tree," he said –
and then we caught sight of a glimpse of red.

Then into view came a tiny figure,
not much more than the size of a finger.
We gasped our surprise, and froze straight away,
willing the little figure to stay.

He bowed, and jumped high in the air.
And we suddenly realised it was a small bear.
The old man was grinning from ear to ear,
as we wanted to learn all we could hear.

The bears, it appeared, came from a far distant land, and
had found our tree just warm and grand.
They welcomed our friendship with delight, and
said no more would they walk by night.

Symphony of the Trees

Standing alone, the tree, in all its winter finery,
could look and see the scenery
Of other trees, standing stark and bare,
As they, too, looked and could compare
That winter held each one in her icy snare.

The children laugh and run around,
causing snowflakes to fall upon frozen ground.
But listen now, there is water trickling;
the thaw has come at last
To reclaim the trees from their winter mantle fast.

Buds are bursting through, on still snow-clad branches,
last to shed their load.
It's free of winter; now we can begin
To blossom forth in all our glory to another spring.
Awake, you mighty oaks, and sing as,
by thrusting your branches to the sky,
You, too, will relive the joys of other countless springs,
When bursting buds and shiny leaves appear,
We're on our way to say that summer's here.

The joy of seeing the trees in all their splendour,
Robed with beauty and delight,
rendering of another song of pleasure.
We can only stand and stare,
wondering at the change we see around us.
But as time rolls by we must say
farewell to the beauty we see.

Leaves are changing again to russet and gold,
And autumn winds blow the leaves from the trees.
Only one Creator could make the colours so bold
That they claim the senses of all who behold.

The Cat

*Aloof and alone, the black cat stalks the darkening streets,
pushing aside rubbish in his search for a meal.
He finds what he wants in packaging real.*

*Hark now! A new sound is heard in the street.
The black cat ventures to meet
the meanest of adversaries.
With hackles rising and claws intent
on inflicting punishment on the intruder.*

*As the black cat coils to spring
the stranger, too, prepares – and swings
in a dangerous manner to oppose the king.*

*As the howls of the sparring two meet
a hush falls over the neighbourhood,
awaiting, with bated breath,
the outcome of the fight to the death.*

*Suddenly the intruder, punished enough,
slinks away into the night to lick his wounds –
and think he's tough.
The black cat also licks his wounds –
and wanders away along the street.
He's lived through the danger he had to beat,
and gave of himself, like a soldier brave,
who will live to fight another day.*

Sea Mist

With the boats drawn alongside the old harbour wall,
The captains wait to hear the call –
The unearthly baying of the Sussex hounds,
Where Eddie and Jake could be found.

A harvest moon glides silently across the sky,
Whereupon an animal utters a heart-rending cry.
All around, the shadows can be seen,
To terrorise the lonesome figures that once had been.

Suddenly a different sound is heard –
A high-pitched whistle, replacing the spoken word.
The captains hastily prepare their boats,
Bringing them around so they could float
Off-shore the island, like a shrouded coat.

The minutes tick away and nothing moves;
It's as though Eddie and Jake had been removed.
Again the animal cry rends the air,
Bringing panic to the hunted pair.

As their time of freedom draws quickly to a close,
We watch with bated breath to see them pose,
Exposed in the lights of the boats along the harbour wall.
And, as they are arrested, their deeds done,
We have them trapped, and indeed outrun.

Imagine

Imagine dewdrops on the petal of a rose,
Then imagine a scene that everyone knows:
Say, skaters on a rink of ice;
And you'll have a picture that is clear and concise.

If you let your imagination run wild,
It can bear fruit, just like a child.
All kinds of images can transpire,
Bringing depths of wonderment to inspire.

Often we imagine how life would have been
In centuries gone by, but by us unseen.
Would our lives be very different from now,
And would we still be asking how?

I often imagine I'm soaring aloft
On wings that glide, and are so soft;
As I glance down at the earth I've left
I know no fear, nor am I bereft.

How powerful can be our imagery,
That nothing may appear what it seems.
We've come close to losing our status quo,
And come very close to our dreams.

Enquiring and imaginative minds
Can lead to inventions of many kinds.
They fuel the thoughts of scientific men
Who are glad to prove their powers of acumen.

IMAGINATION
is everything

Ronnie the Mule

*Ronnie the mule was playing the fool
as he fell off his perch and into the pool.
It wiped the smile off his face, but he was cool,
and he decided to play by the golden rule.*

*It took him a while to bring back a smile
but then he decided he would run a mile.
The route was set, as was the pile
of shoes; Ronnie wanted to climb the stiles.*

*Over the fields and streams went Ronnie,
proud as punch, happy and bonny.
We watch our little mule as he turns to be funny,
and laugh with him, as he makes lots of money.*

*Now Ronnie has a friend called Bunny,
who's a fully-grown rabbit, and very funny.
With the money he made Ronnie will bring
our funny rabbit to live with him.*

*The pair lived together for many a year,
and got on so well that there was never a tear.*

FIREWORKS

"My goodness" – it's November all over again,
And time to take stock of the 'Golden Rain'.
Fireworks a-plenty in the shops,
So now is the time to check the box.

Catherine Wheels, and Sparklers, too –
There's plenty about for me and you.
Rockets sent spiralling into the sky
Bring forth "Oohs", "Ahs" and "Oh, my!"

The bonfire is ready, and so is the guy,
When both of them will reach for the sky.
Cold hands are warmed by the blaze of the fire,
And chestnuts are roasted in the pyre.

Potatoes are baked by zealous Mums,
To fill ready-and-waiting hungry tums.
The feast is over, as a guitar is strummed,
And hot chocolate, bath, and bed are summoned.

Minnie the Mouse

Minnie the mouse kept a very neat house.
As she dusted and polished until everything gleamed.
Her pride in her home became over-esteemed.
She kept a fine larder, with everything there,
But never invited her friends to take fare.

Shutting herself away one day
She was saddened and lonely, as was her way.
"Oh my", she cried, "What shall I do?
My friends have all deserted me too".

"I know what to do," says Minnie.
"I'll buy some cheese and plenty of bread,
And invite my friends for supper instead."

This was accepted with a great "Hooray"
And everyone said it had been a good day.
Now Minnie has friends sharing her home
And never thinks to winge or moan,
As she settles down comfortably without a groan.

Mildred the Duck

Pecking around in the farm-yard,
Mildred the duck became bored.
She wanted to see the outside world,
That her Mother had told her about.
She flew around in the dust,
Kicking up quite a fuss,
Until the farmer arrived and opened the gate.

Quickly Mildred flew out, at such a great rate
That she gave no thought to her pining mate.
Squawking and running, she covered some ground,
Until hunger told her there must be food around.
But, "Oh, dear me, no" the gate was shut.
There would be no going back for Mildred the duck.

Cat Nap

Snoozing quietly by the fire,
The tabby cat's dream may be swift and dire:
Is it a mouse, or maybe a morsel
That twitches those whiskers of the damsel?

A tiny me-ow issues from the mouth of the cat,
So all may know this is where she's at.
The dog looks away, with a scornful sigh,
And waits to get closer to the fire, by and by.

The sleeper sleeps on, blissfully unaware
She's the centre of attention, so dogs beware!
Suddenly a paw flashes out and catches an imaginary mouse,
En route to its nest in the rear of the house.

Some dreams may be nightmares of a sort,
As she quivers and twitches as though caught
By a pack of baying hounds
That for her life they knew no bounds.

The children gently stroke her coat of fur
As from deep within her body, comes a gentle purr.
Awake now and stretching, she surveys her world,
With tail slowly wagging and body uncurled.

It's time for a snack, as she moves to her bowl,
After which she elegantly proceeds to roll.
With her cat nap over, she shakes a paw
And promptly wanders off next door.

Teddy Bear Blues

Out from the pram the teddy bear fell,
as he was thrown out by his owner, Mel.
From between the pram wheels he escaped,
and lay there for a while, considering his fate.

Up on chubby legs he stands,
to look around and see he's stranded.
A large black dog barks as he goes by,
frightening our teddy, who asks why
he should be here upon the ground,
instead of the safety of the pram.

Running along in the gutter,
he sees a ball, and starts to mutter.
Kicking the ball this way and that,
he begins to think it doesn't matter
that he's lost and away from Mel.

When suddenly, a pram he spies,
and, as he opens both his eyes,
he's scooped up from the ground
and hugged by Mel ecstatically.
So our little lost bear finds his way home,
where he vows that never again will he roam.

Little Brown Rabbit

Oh little brown rabbit, where are you going,
with your tail a-bobbing
and your ears a-blowing?
A basket in your hand, I see;
is what's in it something nice for tea?

Who are you having in today?
Is it someone you know and who wants to play?
Little brown rabbit, you are so caring,
so much, but not over-bearing.

You look after all those in need,
which can tell others to take some heed.
With your basket of goodies,
you tell others where the food is,
and invite them to come in with a kiss.

I hope, Little Brown Rabbit,
someone will look after you one day,
inviting you in,
in their own dear way.

Eagle Eyes

*Wheeling and dipping in its search for a meal
The magnificent eagle glides through the air.
Proudly, on wings spread wide, she spots a likely prey and dives.*

*Sporting the catch, she ascends to her eyrie home
High up on the mountain crags.
The eaglets are hungry; that is why she must pacify their needs today.
What a scramble in the nest, each hoping to get the best,
But mother knows their every need, and, reaching down, she shares alike,
So all get fed, to their delight.*

*Once more she soars towards the skies.
This time a rabbit catches her eye.
With precision timing she swoops to the ground,
Where the eaglets' next meal would be found.*

*Tired after hunting from morn to night,
She retires to her nest to have a short respite.
No rest for her, though, her young agree.
Again on the wing to avert the need
She soars and glides above the ground,
Watching and listening for the slightest sound.*

*Eagerly the eaglets await the return of their parent,
Anticipating a handsome share-out;
Worn out and weary, she at last settles in the nest,
Preparing for the next day's test.*

Dancing Feet

Tap, tap, tap on the wooden floor
danced the feet, to the count of four,
tapping and toeing in a graceful dance –
was close to putting us into a trance.

As the music slowed, so the feet stood still,
waiting expectantly for the thrill
of performing again, as, with bated breath,
they took up the story of Macbeth.

The orchestra took up another score,
which set the feet dancing some more.
Whirling and leaping in perfect timing -
it could hardly be said that they were miming!

As the music echoed and echoed around the stage,
it seemed the feet were in a daze
of interpreting the sounds into a dance,
demanding much more than a glance.

As the music faded, the dancing ceased.
It certainly had been much more than a feast.
Then, to the roar of the audience's applause,
the feet started tapping again on the floor.

The music rose in crescendo, and the feet were off.
It seemed as if they would never stop.
They were encored and encored again and again,
but to the dancing feet it was not in vain.

At last the performance came to an end,
with a leap and a thrust and a final spin.
The curtain came down, as oft it would,
and we stood spellbound, as only we could.

Pepe

I have a cat called Pepe; she really is a dear.
She leaps from branch to fence, without any fear.
Her exploits vary and are very many.
How she manages the games she invents
Is really quite uncanny.

Something large descends on my chest while I am asleep.
It's only Pepe, come to play a game of hide and seek.
She settles down beside me, with a very gentle mew,
And pretty soon we're both asleep, until the morning dew.

It's fun having Pepe as a live-in guest;
She's taken over my life, and now I never rest
From playing games with Pepe, who always gives her best.
She rushes around the furniture as her feelings are expressed.

Papers to skid on are not a chore,
As Pepe spreads them all over the floor.
She loves to play with her many toys,
And amuses my grandchildren one girl, four boys.
An elasticated spider is her main delight,
As we watch, bemused, at her paws so sleight.

Friendship

A friend in need is a friend indeed, how often have we heard
This popular English saying, afresh in every word?
To be a friend is the greatest compliment one can ever bestow,
Where there's no need to utter words, but simply there to know.

How quietly, how gently a friend will come upon a need
And whisper words of comfort, to watch that pain recede.
Shared joys and sorrows, emotions, too,
Will keep that friendship alive for you.

Friendships take time to build, bringing harvests of delight,
When talk is plentiful, and faces with pleasure alight.
We need to find mutual thoughts and understanding,
With age and ethnic culture notwithstanding.

Confidences and secrets can be spoken of by friends,
Whose wise and gentle counsel may lead to sweet amends.
Problems shared are often problems halved,
And often, whilst examining, we've cried and laughed.

To have a special friend, you must be a good friend, too,
That often embraces a wider window with a different view.
These views discussed and in tolerance rest
Will bring forth a friendship of the very best.

*Finally, friendships can be like a cuddly toy
Who's warm and comforting – even for a boy!
They're there to listen to heartfelt joy and pain,
Then, very patiently, will listen again and again.*

Monkey

My old ragged Monkey, so loved and so worn,
Had only one arm, and a leg that was torn.
I trailed him by one arm as off I would trot,
To see if my fingers would fit in the lock.

Monkey went everywhere with me, you see,
Even to coming to sit down for tea.
If I lost myMonkey I would cry bitter tears
Until he was found again, relieving my fears.

We would walk down the path hand in hand –
It seemed like we were a merry band,
As Teddy and Dolly would often come, too,
To provide some ideas of what mischief to do.

Up and down the lane we'd go,
marching onwards, to and fro.
What joyful times we had together,
playing tag, and getting better.

Our days seemed one long holiday,
full of fun and endless play.
We gave it the best that we could muster -
Before school days came in as a joy-buster.

I now hurried home, eager to see my
precious Monkey sitting on my knee.
We made up for lost time by
singing songs and nursery rhymes.

How long the days seemed, as a child;
sunny weather, always mild.
I can rarely remember a rainy day
when we couldn't go outdoors to play.

The years rushed by at a steady rate,
And by now Monkey looked in a terrible state.
His fur was worn, with patches bare,
But still he behaved without a care.

At last came the day when Monkey was relinquished;
It wasn't as if he didn't have a blemish.
Loved as he'd been through the years,
Monkey retained his pose – with both his ears!

The Tiger and the Elephant

"Good morning, Your Highness," the tiger bowed;
"I see you can really stand out in a crowd."
The elephant nodded with cool disdain, and trumpeted,
"I never stand out in the rain."

The tiger backed away as only tigers can,
and, putting on his thinking cap, he came up with a plan:
he would entice the elephant down to the river
and there, he would show him a bow and a quiver.
"That would never pierce my thick side," squealed the elephant,
"so – no more rides."

The tiger knew he had gone far enough,
but he wanted the elephant to think he was tough.
The tiger didn't really want to play rough,
but the elephant had lorded it over him quite long enough.

Next time the trumpet sounded
the animals cringed, and some bounded.
As the elephant came to drink, the tiger rounded
and spoke in a very disrespectful way.
He said His Highness would have to pay
but could still come to the watering hole each day.

No favours would he receive –
and that he was lucky he had a reprieve.
So the elephant, with his head hung down,
said he had learned his lesson, safe and sound –
and was a happier elephant all around.

A Tasty Treat (If I Can Get It?)

I gaze, I yearn, I wonder why;
A tasty treat I can espy.
I grin, and press my nose towards the glass.
This surely cannot be a farce?

My lips pursue the tasty morsel,
On top of which it's becoming crucial
To satisfy this sensual craving
With logical thought that is all prevailing.

Gone is my mind of sweet repose;
Now I languish in the very throes
Of strange desires unsatisfied.
How could I not linger and hurry by?

Delicious smells assail me now
As deep in my thoughts I make a vow.
No more would I wait in patient anticipation –
But play my part in full participation!

I pushed the door of the baker's shop.
It gave an inch – then appeared to stop.
With all my attempts to remain composed –
The shop was very obviously closed!

Head to Head

*"Whisper, whisper, little children, can I share your secret too?
May I listen so intently that I can learn all about you?
I'd like to listen to your laughter when you tell a favourite friend
That you'll be her friend for ever, never ever without end."*

*"Heads together in the playground; is it just a hoax?
Or do you need a bevy of friends that you can gently coax?
Do you have signals too, as we have in the adult world,
Or are they being gently matured, as yet to be unfurled?"*

*"What about those children standing shyly by the wall;
Can we bring them in to play, or will that not do at all?
Why are they on the fringe of having friendships made?
Have they upset you, or perhaps not made the grade?"*

*"Can you protect these lonely ones from bullying, for sure;
Maybe just enough to comfort and reassure?
Broken-hearted children are the broken adults of tomorrow,
So every touch and smile you give prevents them so much sorrow."*

*"I understand your peer pressure is very strong at school,
But maybe you need to make your own up and disregard their rule.
Friendships formed now can be precious ones for life,
Supporting in the hardest times, but never causing strife."*

*"So, as head to head together you plan and so conspire
An agreement that now will very soon transpire
Into a full and certain happening of events within your control,
To offer the underlings a sure and certain role."*

Distant Lands

Eastern beaches, southern shores –
Name our destination, preferred.
Mountain crags or slippery slopes
Are dazzling with our plans and hopes.
Brochures scoured,
Thoughts empowered;
Mindful of the days and hours.
Careful selection of each location
Can be, to us, an endless vocation.
Daydreaming of a place to visit
May not always be so exquisite.
Elephant trips into jungle clearing
May not, to you, sound very appealing.
It's great for travellers who are not so shy
That they can't wait for night, to see the fireflies.
But, if this is too daunting a prospect,
There are many more places you can inspect:
Mediterranean islands, soft balmy breezes,
Are tempting as any that allures and pleases.
So our choice is made
And expenses paid –
It's off to sample, and the moment of truth,
To relax and enjoy the return to our youth.

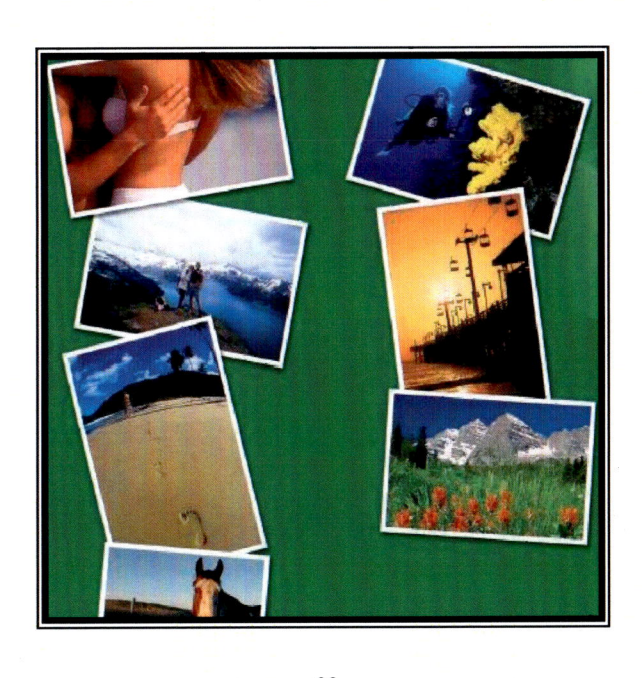

The Sweet Shop

Gob-stoppers, sherbet dabs, and much, much more,
Are arrayed behind the sweet shop's door.
Maltesers, chocolate drops and liquorice, too,
With a lot of choice for me and you.

I think my favourites were the strawberry bon-bons,
That in my childhood required two coupons.
These coupons were issued as part of rationing,
Which, after the war, gave rise to de-rationing.

Though some foods were scarce after the war,
There was always one sweet shop that opened its door
To children, on their way to school,
And when friendship was the golden rule.

I remember the counter, crammed full of sweets;
I really didn't know which ones to eat.
I would select a few, then change my mind;
To be so undecided was a great bind.

Now today's sweets are much more refined,
And, as well as holiday rock, you will find
A sweet or chocolate to suit every young Brit,
From coconut mushrooms to banana split.

Walnut whips, Galaxy, Crunchie, and Mars,
Lemon drops, candy, and all in the jars,
Become one big shop of fabulous sweets,
That it's hard to know another it couldn't beat.

The Supermarket Trolley

Stacked in lines – what a find;
To discover one suitable; that's not a bind.
Some with frames and some with seats,
And some with pedal cars at your feet!

Some run smoothly and some run rough,
But don't despair if the going's tough –
We all know the idiosyncrasies of the supermarket trolley
That spin on their wheels – what a folly!

With children in tow for the shopping trip,
It's "all hands on the trolley with a tight grip"
As we waltz down the aisles with a determined stride.
Our shopping lists and money keep us occupied.

It always amazes me to see
How differently filled a trolley can be.
Some goods are placed neatly, row by row,
Allowing little room for muddle to grow.

Others are so piled high with food
That all sorts of interesting things protrude.
Shopping's been thrown in, willy-nilly,
That the trolley bounces along merrily.

Whilst pulled up at the checkouts, our goods we surrender
To the scrutiny of the price tags, making us big spenders.
With a sigh and "well done" we relax in the car;
We've survived the ordeal, and got us this far!

The Steam Train

Clickity-clack, clickity-clack hurries the train along the track,
With smoke billowing forth from its tall chimney stack.
The steam train races along the Hog's Back,
Towards the tunnel large and black.

As we approach the tunnel the train gives a whistle,
Loud and long, rather like a steam kettle.
It was impressive to hear, and rather shrill,
But never-the-less it gave us a thrill.

The fast train from Paddington was always on time,
Even though we were going to the end of the line.
The mighty wheels pounded the track so proudly,
Taking us home to a place welcoming and lively.

In its compartments so regally upholstered,
Each seat had its armrest and white linen bolster.
Outside in the corridors so long and so narrow,
We rattled along as straight as an arrow.

With pistons pumping and coal fires burning,
The wheels of the locomotive kept on turning.
Soot wafts in through the windows from the engine up front –
Though the coal used in this furnace you can no longer confront.

With two drivers in the cab so strong and so brawny,
And with fire-shovelling shift-work they were far from scrawny.
These drivers in the cab came under strict scrutiny
To keep us on time to get home for tea.

The Library Book

On a shelf in the library I sat for a year,
While books all around me would laugh and jeer.
I was unwanted, unloved and ashamed
That nobody wanted to call me by name.

My pages were curled and my cover looked dim,
As I decided my fate was incredibly grim.
I sat forlornly, day by day,
And nobody came to take me away.

The story within my bound pages
Contained exploits of kings and of sages;
They told of an exciting, daring plan,
That with love and joy the world had sang.

When deep and hurt in my despair
A small child had come out of nowhere;
He lifted me up with trembling hands
And carried me off to his homelands.

This child was a prince of great renown
And had a kingdom of his own.
He and his father ruled justly and well,
And of their greatness I could tell.

As I settled into my new-found home,
I knew I would never want to roam.
My life in the library was just a bad dream
And nothing anywhere may be quite what it seems.

The Settee

The old brown settee was lumpy and worn;
its arms and chair-backs had long been torn.
A long time ago its colour had faded,
and now it felt rather rejected and jaded.

The Father and Mother of the house
had bought it twenty years before.
From then on it had seen service galore.
Visitors were ushered to sit on its cushions plump,
with never a question of there being a lump.

With four children now in the house,
no-one was as quiet as a mouse.
The settee loved all the attention it got
with its place by the fire, comfortably hot.

As the children left home, only two remained.
Now courting days were the thing of the present,
And the settee looked forward to each visit.
As the couple gleefully clung together,
so the settee decided it was very "with it".

Now there was only one child at home,
who had no inclination to roam.
The settee was sagging a little by now,
but was determined to cling on and how.

This youngest child was beginning to knit
And bounced the old settee about quite a bit.
Its covers loosened and flew about like a kite,
Whilst the settee clung on with all his might.

Worn, but loved, the settee into the playroom was moved.
Its covers had long ago been removed,
but now it had a kind of reprieve;
The youngest child had something up her sleeve!

One by one, all her dolls and toys were on the settee sat.
Then began the business of bandaging,
as the settee smelt a rat.
It was the beginning of the "hospital era" when its
lease of life would stretch out further.
The settee enjoyed the new adventure,
which gave way to a reprieve on censure.

With its head held high, and with no more than a sigh,
The settee finally came to its resting place,
Knowing it had run a great race.
He went to join his peers in the sky,
Earning his gold reward by and by.

The Rocking Horse

Galloping across the carpeted plain,
little Roy Rogers rides again.
With his trusty steed beneath his feet,
this cowboy will never think of defeat.

Bullet after bullet pumps into the store.
It's the "Crazy Gang" as has never been seen before.
Little Johnny pushes his horse to the limit;
he shoots one bandit down onto the floor,
as he prepares to take on some more.

As his mind works overtime,
the scene changes again,
and, as the cheer of the crowd rings in his ears,
The spectators had eliminated all fears.

Over the water jump; "this is easy," sighs Johnny,
urging his horse into" top gear"
to jump the high wall. Wow! That's some feat –
but Johnny will never think of defeat.

As he slowly canters around the arena,
he knows he has a few to beat.
Lining up now for the moment of truth,
on and on he gallops his horse –
and the jump is cleared; and there's the proof.

The awe-inspiring high wall, still with its roof,
as the crowd roars; they love him so.
His mother calls him: "Johnny, it's time to go."
Reluctantly he dismounts from his horse,
promising again another ride on the course.

The Smallest Sparrow

Waiting his turn with his brothers and sisters to be fed,
little Henry always felt unhappy – and red.
His feathers, you see, had not really grown ,
leaving his wings almost colourless when they should have been brown.

His father knew how unhappy he was
and suggested a remedy for his youngest son.
He would make Henry a special coat.
Then he would fly through the air with the greatest of ease,
and no more would his brothers and sisters tease.

Henry was happy and jumped up and down;
his feathers would once again be brown.

Whilst his father worked hard on the coat,
Henry was naughty, and could only gloat.
His mother at this point made her plea:
Henry would get nothing for tea until he learnt to be repentant,
and be thankful to his parent.
The coat was completed in double-quick time,
and all agreed it was perfect, in twine.

As the youngsters launched themselves into the air,
Henry was able to join them, which was only fair.
Circling and gliding around the nest,
Henry certainly gave his best.
So, thanks to his father, he obtained his wings –
and you know, now, why this little sparrow sings!

Tiptoe Down the Stairs

The Christmas tree stands with branches so fine,
With baubles and tinsel, and smelling of pine;
The garlands of green look so serene,
And in the fireplace there's a magical scene.

A glass of wine and a mince pie
Had been laid out for Santa, and, by and by,
Carrots laid alongside, of the very best,
For Rudolph or Prancer along with the rest.

The food was gone – of that we were sure,
And we knew, somehow, not out of the door.
Soot was spattered on the carpet green,
And the mince pie was a mere has-been!

Descending the staircase tread by tread,
(It's very naughty, we should be in bed!)
There in profusion on the carpeted floor
Lay a mound of presents nearly up to the door.

With pulses a-racing and with bated breath,
Down the stairs we tumbled, expecting certain death.
Our voices were muffled, as were our feet,
And in the silence you could almost hear a heartbeat.

Down on our knees in front of the pile;
It was hard not to laugh or even smile.
Our fingers stroked the elegant wrappings,
And for a preview we were itching.

From out of our reverie we reluctantly came,
To return and mount the stairs again,
As we tiptoed quietly back to our beds
To excitedly await Christmas Day ahead.

A Bedtime Prayer

Holy Jesus, with the gentleness of a child
    I give my life to you, to whom I yield.

    As I sleep this night, in a bed so cosy and warm,
        I know in your presence I can come to no harm.

Holy Jesus, please help those who are in despair
        and make their problems easier to bear.

    Thank you, Holy Jesus, for your perfect rest;
        and grant me love of the very best.

The Frog and the Fairy

Sitting alone on his leaf one day,
a beautiful creature came his way.
The frog, in excitement, gave a loud croak,
which frightened the fairy as she spoke.

"Come and sit with me, please, on my lily leaf,"
begged the frog.
"I won't frighten you again off the log."
The fairy agreed and, in all her beauty, flew towards him,
as the frog's eyes filled to the brim.
"How could I have hurt her?" cried the frog.
"I'll ask her to marry me, if she would."

As they sat together, sunning themselves,
the fairy spoke, as was herself:
"Dear frog," she whispered through her tears,
"I cannot marry you as one of your peers.
It would not be allowed by the Wedding Council;
I would be evicted as a naughty damsel."

"Never mind," said the frog with a hefty sigh,
"we'll elope together, by and by.
I love you, dear fairy, and I can only plea,
you'll love me as much as I love thee."

Abreast of the Times

How sadly we mourn the passing of the years,
But, standing the test of time, they were relinquishing all fears.
How fast did the penicillin grow upon the petri dish,
While trawler-men were bringing us our fish?

The harnessing of electricity was a major feat
And one which, even today, is very hard to beat.
When today's modern railway became the new invention
It gave us scope to travel without intervention.

Transporting goods by horse-drawn barges
Was the means of freight discharges.
They paved the way for waterways and canals
That preceded the days of road and rails.

Our shipping navigation of today is of the very best,
With "ship to shore" and "radar" relaying a request.
Container ships can carry so much refrigeration
That fruit and fish can reach our shores with no deterioration.

The Chelsea Physic Garden of our yesteryear
Is still where shrubs and herbs are grown to help us to prepare
For the discovery of modern medicines to come upon the scene;
Some to soothe the heart, and others important vaccines.

Today we have long laser beams of light
Piercing the darkness, till everything is bright.
Space-stations encircle us at a fantastic speed of flight,
Absorbing information to check that everything's all right.

As our amazing technology becomes so much more advanced,
So our mobile phones and televisions become enhanced.
The scope is wide, the future's always changing,
Therefore the past and today are seen to be exchanging.

The Enchanted Garden

Away from the house, and above the lawns,
Lies a special place, where once adorned,
a summer's day in all its beauty dawned.
Cascading creepers spread over the wall,
but nothing answered to its call.
No blackbirds sang, no sparrows twittered.
Time stands still as if to rule.

This golden rule had been set in place
for the garden to be hidden from those of every race.
A message grim was marked on the door
for those bold enough, but wanting more.
It sent a shiver through the spine,
like tangled foliage so entwined.

With nothing growing, and nothing moving,
This garden held a secret deep, and one it meant to keep.
There is one way by which an entry can be made:
If the old and rusty key would turn and weep,
its job finished, as it held back intruders,
For hundreds of years of sleep.

As the door was opened and nervously entered,
such was a fragrance of pure delight as we ventured in.
Birds and butterflies in flight had become frozen under censure.
A couple stand together in a warm embrace;
They are very still, with no soft breeze to set its pace.

A curse had been set in the garden,
when two young lovers had wanted to marry.
There was to be no reprieve until a pardon broke the spell,
or someone entered
The forbidden sanctuary.

As if in a dream the garden stirred,
as it awoke from its penury.
A lark high up in the sky sang gladly,
setting the scene for this year's century.
As the mists of time rolled the curtains back,
there came murmuring a-plenty:
"We don't know how long we've been in this position,"
sighed the lovers,
Who roused against all opposition.

As tree and flower, birds and bees awoke,
there came a new birth, as from one who spoke.
In a dizzy display of activity
the garden came to life for all to see.
As leaves and petals fluttered to the ground,
the laws by which the garden was bound
Gave up their hold, freeing all that was past.
As the garden was there, so it disappeared,
Gathered upwards into clouds,
from where it had magically appeared.

The Little Red Train

Whee, whee, whistled the little red train,
As he chuffed round and round on his track again.
This was fun and he could always agree
That this was where he would like to be.

Then, off the tracks he came to ride
Across bumpy cushions that had no glide.
He wobbled a bit from side to side,
Rather like being on a slippery slide.

Riding now on floors so bare;
Down in the gully and up in the air.
His master was happy in his play,
But for the train it was just another day.

Asleep at last on the young boy's pillow,
The train was glad he wasn't brilliant yellow.
Red trains had so much more fun,
Even if he was the only one.

... And So They Came

The people came from near and far, together as a crowd.
They came to listen to a man whose voice, though gentle, spoke out loud.
To a hillside in Judea was their destination,
As they trod the road with dogged determination.

The paths were rough, strewn with stones and boulders,
And many carried weak and weary ones upon their shoulders,
This man, they knew, this Jesus could call down blessings from on high,
And preached a strange new message that could only satisfy.

And so they came to listen to the man whose name was spread abroad.
Little did they know His name was "Lord".
All who came, even those furthermost in the crowd,
Could clearly hear His words, as they would cover and enshroud.

Blind men, beggars, lepers were all upon the hill,
But when Jesus spoke, the mind was strangely still.
As new ground was covered, and with every heart a-race,
The people came to recognise the Saviour of the human race.

Touched by Jesus' teaching and His human appeal,
Many people in the crowd found they had been healed.
Laughing, crying, thankfully they came
To bring homage to this Saviour they had not known by name.

Jesus had filled their yearning hearts
With a divine message that imparts
A reconciliation for today, with a brand new start
Of a relationship with God who will never depart.

The Scarecrow

"Away with you, you pesky crows,
Who eat the corn the farmer grows".
The scarecrow's lament wafted into the air,
Doing little to distract or scare.

With straw for his hands and straw for his feet,
The scarecrow found it hard to beat
Those adversaries who so liked to preen
Their feathers, in mockery, to a bright sheen.

Day after day he stood his ground,
Trying desperately to move his arms around.
Then some children called over the hedge,
"Hi, scarecrow, you look all on edge."

This annoyed the scarecrow so
That he determined to ask his good friend, Mo.
Mo was a field mouse, small and sprightly,
With two little black eyes that shone so brightly.

She came up with a brilliant idea
To tie some coloured ribbons into his hair.
As she worked and wove for all the crows to see,
She almost missed going home for tea.

As the breeze got up and the ribbons fluttered,
The crows stayed away, as many muttered,
"It's all very well for scarecrow's friend,
But we need to eat the corn again."

"Oh no, you don't," said the scarecrow bravely,
"We can always make the ribbons wavy.
That will scare the lot of you,
And we'll start right now without more ado."

The Rocking Chair

The rocking chair, so quiet and serene,
Had many, many years of service seen.
The covers on its seat were now, not so neat,
But the texture of the wood was still hard to beat.

Old Granny Smith had been its first owner,
Making with it, her own persona.
The family would gaze through the bedroom door,
Watching Granny rocking more and more.

When Granny died,
The rocking chair was put to one side.
Its new owners came to live in the house,
By which time the chair had been claimed by a mouse.

With its drapery thoroughly bitten and torn,
The poor rocking chair seemed very forlorn.
By now it faced an uncertain future,
Filled only now with conjecture.

Every day seemed so much the same,
As the magic of the rocking chair began to wane.
Then suddenly a child appeared in the house
And the old rocking chair began to arouse.

One day the child climbed onto the old rocking chair
And, rocking backwards and forwards, golden light fell from his hair.
It was a blissful moment for them both,
As the old rocking chair suddenly felt new growth.

The following day the Mother appeared,
And, with her son, sat on the chair.
As they rocked to and fro
The rocking chair took on a brand new glow.

They moved the chair to a prominent place
From where he could see every smiling face.
His life was no longer sad and dreary,
But vigorous, loved – and in no way weary.

My Hottie

My hot water bottle is a big cuddly bear,
My closest companion, which is only fair.
I drag him around the house by day,
And at night, snug in my bed, he's tucked away.

Filled with hot water 'til he's nice and fat,
I often sit with "bear" on my lap.
He has a cover that's soft and smooth,
And if I'm upset, will gently soothe.

My dreams are sweeter when hottie's there
As I fall asleep without a care.
My toes are warm and cosy, too,
And without my hottie I wouldn't know what to do.

When a bad ache or pain brings no clemency,
Then hottie's there with the remedy,
Placed nice and warm on the aching part,
And in a short while the pain you'll outsmart.

My hottie's left alone when it's time to go out,
And I often wonder if he would pout.
No sooner than I'm home I cuddle him again,
And gaze out of the window at the persistent rain.

Slipped into bed, nice and warm, before to sleep I go,
I can tell my hottie my deepest woe.
His face benignly searches mine,
And I'm reassured everything is fine.

The Deliciously Amusing, Fang-toothed Cat

Lying like a panther in the new-mown hay,
the fang-toothed cat nearly gave his game away;
he's a rake.
Like a snake.
What mischief can he make?

Up a tree. Can he make it home for tea?
Dashing, jaunty, full of fun;
from him all other cats will run.

Black and sleek, our cat will beat
all the others in the street.
He's good-looking, handsome and bold;
of him many tales can be told.

As he searches in the undergrowth,
his body stiffened for all its worth,
paws getting dirty in the earth,
he finds what he's looking for,
and bats it with a wayward paw.

Something alerts our fang-toothed cat;
I wonder if it's a rat?
Hackles rising,
body bristling
heart a-racing
our cat wonders what he's chasing.
Danger's over – he's in control,
and promptly decides to have a roll.

We'll leave this black cat for a moment,
and wait awhile, to see his opponent.

He's gone to sleep in the new-mown hay,
and there we'll leave him for another day.

The Dressing-up Box

*Silent and forlorn, the dressing-up box stood
next to the dolls' house, made of wood.
They had long been despatched to the attic floor,
whereby they would be seen no more.*

*"Not so," said the cutest doll that could be;
"I see bright days ahead for you and me.
The children have grown, of that I agree;
but their children will come running, just you see."*

*Then the medieval lady, mermaid and nurse
will come to life, as in the verse.
Black diamond necklaces will glitter again,
as the children seek out no two outfits the same.*

*Games will be invented by clever young minds,
and friendships are formed, that flourish and bind.
Children's voices will be heard, in excitement shrill,
as words are carried on the breeze, shouting "Brill!"*

*No more will the dressing-up box be alone and sad,
when inside its depths many games can be had.
Excited and happy at so much attention,
the dressing-up box totally forgets to mention
the other toys, now out of detention.*

*So here we leave this merry throng,
happy as Larry all day long.
The years have stripped the cobwebs away
As they all have fun, and want to stay.*

The Dandelion Clock

The fluffy white seeds of the dandelion flower
Are blown gently away on the summer breeze,
Like a gentle fairy's pirouette
Lightly, delicately balancing in mid-air
They float, they tumble through space,
Then coming gently down onto the soft earth.
The dandelion clock was well known to me as a child.
Carefully breaking the stem of the flower,
We cradled it wonderingly in our hands.
So delicate and soft.
Blow, blow, our lips with mingled air would sigh.
"One o'clock, two o'clock, three o'clock, four"
We would chant,
As the little white balls of down flew away.
Where they came to rest we did not know –
Only that the tiny seeds would find rest in the soft soil
And, one day soon, a carpet of yellow dandelions
Would bloom again.

The Rock-pool

Growing-up days were spent on the beach,
while everything else was out of reach.
We lived very near the sea, you see,
and practically every day I would shout for glee
as we headed southward on the bus, for free.

Swimming in the sea was no big deal,
as all I wanted were the rock-pools real.
There my imagination would run riot
as I protected my pool from the wicked pirate.

Seaweed left from the ebbing tide
was a perfect place in which to hide
for the small fishes, left high and dry
by the receding waves.

At the bottom of the pool there are crabs to be found,
and sea anemones are around;
limpets, too, cling to the weathered rock –
to prise them off is like dealing with locks!

Winkling and shrimping were my favourite pastime
when dabbling in the rock-pool.
There's a wealth of things to see,
all without breaking the golden rule
of putting things back where they are found,
not upsetting the ecology that is sound.

*The tide turns and claims the rock-pool back
into the ebb and flow of the sea without check.
I stand in the sands, with bare feet,
and allow the waves and the currents to meet.*

*With fishing rod and bucket, I travel home
to relate my tale of the pirate bold,
and get ready for the next time when I roam
on to the rocks again, with water cold.*

The Tooth Fairy

Hovering quietly around the bed,
the Tooth Fairy herself had said,
"As they dream the dream of dreams,
the tooth under the pillow I shall redeem."
It once was in a mouth so small
it really couldn't hold them all;
so one by one the tiny baby teeth were shed
and placed under the pillow for the fairy instead.
She always came as a result of a call
from the Chief of the Fairies Overall.
As each fairy spent time by every boy and girl,
she would sing a melody as pure as a pearl.
This melody would soothe the sleeper
into a beautiful sleep that went much deeper.
The Tooth Fairy always had plenty of money
to put under the pillows with the sweetness of honey.
She knew these children, from homes so poor,
that she always gave a little more.
The fairies are busy every night
and rarely have time for any respite.
The collected teeth are, by magic, turned to gold,
which, like star dust, is given sevenfold
to boys and girls all over the world
as magic petal dust, beautifully furled.
This brings to the sleeper a perfume so fine
that sweet dreams with the aroma gently entwine.

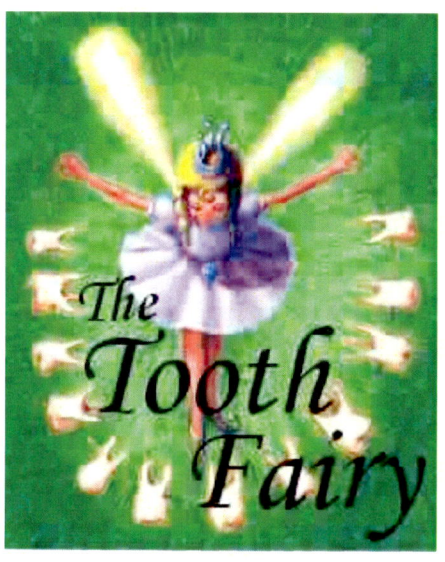

Daisy Bright

Daisy bright, daisy bright,
The source of those who give delight;
You're full of light
In your summer white.
As with red poppies you invite,
Beautiful vistas we can enjoy.
As with beauty you adorn the fields,
So that each has a different countenance.
A gentle breeze blows through the fields,
Rippling the flowers with poise and elegance;
The joy of seeing the meadows so full of promise
That senses are roused,
And we look to the time when man shall see the fields
And praise God for His majesty.

Playtime

*Oh the joy of harmless play,
when children learn social skills each day.
They interact with friends at school,
learning how to keep the rule.*

*At home with siblings, young or old,
emerges a child who is confident and bold.
There are many ways to entertain,
to give another pleasure; and remain
an unspoilt child all the same.*

*Happy days and merry ways
make for peaceful, fulfilled days.
Running around on the football pitch
makes for fun without a hitch.
When a goal is scored, wow, what a thrill,
and all the other children think it's "brill!"*